SELF-LOVE JOURNAL

A journey to inner peace and happiness

AKAL PRITAM

Dear Soul,

May you surrender to self-love, the blooming of your joyful heart, as you journey towards more inner peace and happiness.

Imagine that as your sweetness, your fragrance — the essence of YOU — is beckoned to release, a sacred rose opens in your heart space.

May you choose to give ultimate power to your heart and soul instead of the mind, letting your own inner wisdom lead to your creative destiny.

May you journey gently with your feet firmly in reality, for this sovereign work deserves real time and space. Self-devotion to self-realise is invaluable.

May you discover many inner wisdom pearls and enchanting jewels of self when you dive into this journey.

May you come to understand there is no right or wrong, good or bad, just stories we perceive and tell during an earth-bound, celestial dance between the forces of nature.

May you understand that it's your birthright to record your own invocations and personal love story to then experience. You might consider that it is very healthy for your stability to keep changing, as in this way you will be guided to find balance and who you are at the centre of existence — your true self.

May you love yourself through the process of transformation, not judge yourself and stop the inner blooming. I encourage you to keep unfurling to your pure heart's sweetness.

May you wisely say goodbye to many things on this journey, as acknowledging and honouring necessary goodbyes is a very powerful step on the journey of self-love.

I believe self-love is very personal so I encourage you to add your own art, collaging, drawing and painting through every page along with your writing.

I have divided this journey into the chakras, offering an opportunity to work through these main energy centres as a way to clear out any un-love.

I celebrate your beautiful, creative rhythm.

I bow down to you and thank you for all that you are.

You are invaluable.

With love and gratitude,

Akal.

XOXOXOXO

On this day

I begin my deeper journey of transformation

with self-devotion. I work towards

living completely creatively,

in peace and happiness.

My intention is towards 100 per cent

self-love, respect, forgiveness, compassion

and understanding.

With reverence for my whole life and

whole self — mind, body and soul —

I value progression and steady commitment.

I acknowledge I am a beautiful soul who

deserves to live my creative destiny.

So be it.

Sign here

The new woman is unfurling, a new archetype for a new era.
She is more graceful. She is more radiant. She is always becoming more intuitive.
She patiently waits to be imagined anew. She is fluid — without fear —
in contemporary space. The stream of Adi Shakti carries her far.
Her new self-perception creates a vision to behold. She is becoming more sensory.
She is more soulful. She is the feminine expression of the Aquarian dharma,
bearing sacred water for all, no exclusions.
She brings forth nourishing and nurturing super intelligence.
She leads with love, compassion and sophistication.

You can look
at the Chakra system
as a mapping of how
the mind and body
intersect and how
your emotions live
and intersects in
your body.

Any major trauma
or abuse at certain
stages of your
development will
leave an imprint
on your subtle body.

— 8th Chakra

— 7th Chakra

— 6th Chakra

— 5th Chakra

— 4th Chakra

— 3rd Chakra

— 2nd Chakra

— 1st Chakra

The subtle
energy body,
e-motion.

A self-love journey to happiness and inner peace through healing your chakras.

The centre of your body is a mystical place, and without focused awareness your energy, perception and focus sit outside this inner sanctuary.

In the physical body the spine and nervous system reside in this centre, or at least are designed to be central: strong, flexible and always working to find a balance between all opposites. Left and right, masculine and feminine, sun and moon are a few of the opposites that exist within your experiences.

This central channel is also a conduit for subtle energy, pure creation energy that should be free to ebb and flow through your every moment, regenerating and refreshing your whole mind and body system.

It is believed by many future ancients (awareness practitioners) that along this main energy channel exist vortices or wheels that spin with a concentration of certain frequencies of energy. These centres are also known as the main chakras. The word 'chakra' comes from the Sanskrit word meaning 'wheel' or 'disc'. You may visualise these discs spinning and vibrating as the *prana* (cosmic energy/life force) moves through them. It is also helpful to think of the chakras as gears — ultimately you want to be able to change gears up and down the chakras for your health. Healthy chakras that are clear and balanced, with energy flowing through them, help you to maintain good health, a sense of harmony and clear direction in life.

The chakra system correlates to the major glands of the endocrine, which governs your hormones. A balanced endocrine system has a direct effect on your emotions and thoughts as well as your physical health. The chakra system is also a developmental psychology, from the base of your spine to the crown of your head; from the most basic, foundational aspects of who you are to the more advanced, subtle and skilful aspects of who you are. The normal cycle of life has different phases of development; there are different rites of passage that you go through in your energetic life and different skill sets you develop and refine. Any major trauma, abuse or injury at certain phases of your development has an effect on your subtle energy body. This also includes being subject to environmental toxicity, a poor diet, stress and worry.

The chakras are active all the time, but at certain stages in your life different chakras become the rite of passage. When you work with one chakra you are working with them all. These centres are each part of a whole.

The eight main chakras are:

- root chakra, 0-7 years
- sacral chakra, 8-14 years
- solar plexus chakra, 15-21 years
- heart chakra, 22-28 years
- throat chakra, 29-35 years
- third eye chakra, 36-42 years
- crown chakra, 43-49 years
- aura, from birth

You may choose to work with any chakra section in this journal, going intuitively back and forth, reflecting and creating, to expand your self-compassion and self-forgiveness and find your true pathway to happiness and peace.

Root chakra

First chakra, muladhara, pronounced 'mU-lA-dhA-ra'

Location: perineum, below genitals, base of the spine, the pelvis plexus

Associated body parts: bones, skeletal structure

Related function: adrenals, fight/flight response

Bija mantra, seed sound: LAM

I allow divine nature to move me, to change me. My body is my guardian angel. My breath connects me to my soul. I am supported. I am free to be me. I am here to love my true self.

The root chakra relates to how you see yourself in your surroundings. Before you were born, the orientation of this energy centre determined how your first needs were met. Your nervous system and breathing patterns were developed in the womb and inherited from your mother. You choose your birth mother in order to attune your frequency to attract certain soul lessons into your life. Everything in this life is synchronised and orchestrated on your behalf so that divine energy can be realised through you. However, trauma in the first seven years of life can lead to a belief that you are a victim of circumstance, so that insecurity and fears lead you to seek to control rather than surrender to real personal growth.

To heal this energy centre work with the lens of infinite possibilities, seeing yourself as a wonderful creator born anew in each moment in the here and now. Let the past go by adopting a gratitude practice with a 360 degree eagle's eye view. Practise seeing the bigger picture, releasing any self-aggressive thought patterns that insist you react rather than reflect. Forgive as you contemplate your true heart and self-love. If any memory or situation triggers feelings of blame, shame or complaining, take yourself into your heart and align with Mother Earth's energy, to arrive at your own sweet, full breathing pattern.

A self-loving approach to journalling will ensure you have grounded yourself before you write, never letting the impulses of perceived victimhood or regret guide your pen. Perhaps a helpful place for emotional outpourings is a sheet of paper that in sweet, sacred and personal ceremony you burn. I suggest you save this journal for new creative expression and loving resounding sounds: praise, poetry, dreams, hopes, fresh insights, imaginative intentions and inspiring invocations that you want to live by, concepts that point you clearly in the direction of your creative destiny and true inner peace and happiness.

This section is a great place to articulate your strengths, your beautiful gifts and talents. It is a great place to become your own trusted best friend, never, ever putting yourself down. In a focused state of awareness you will feel grounded and secure, capable and strong, and you will then trust yourself to take the next right action.

From sweet, little things big things grow.

To enjoy the fragrance,
the essence of your life,
your soul ~ connect ♡
make beautiful
connections.
It's time
to regenerate
and
connect
deeply
to your
roots.

Do you smell the roses? Do you know an old tree? Does being in the great mountains move you to cry?
Do you feel your soul beckoning you to sit and converse with Mama Earth?

May I poetically look for beauty. May I embody contentment in the company of fear. May I offer the
magic of hope with my smiling eyes. May I invite conversation through feeling inspired.

With self-love each day you become just a little stronger, more patient, kinder, calmer, wiser and more graceful.

You are free to clear karma this way; you should be your own saviour.

From the deepest roots grows the highest self-esteem; never cut yourself down.

Resurrect yourself, elevate yourself over and over to live the higher destiny of your dharma.

In the valley of patience
she farewelled the material girl.
The mountains called her name.
The passage of infinity
will be crossed this time around.
With two feet upon the ground,
two feet upon the ground.

Everything needed to heal and regenerate is provided in some form in nature.

Dharma is no drama.

Earth prayer

May I learn to work with the element of earth.

May I love the effort of climbing mountains.

May I embrace crossing great distances.

May I see the gifts of all challenges.

May I welcome building strength.

May I uphold courage and compassion.

May I commit to all promises to serve.

May I never, ever give up on visions
of harmony and peace on earth.

May I learn to rely upon miracles.

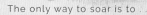

I am free to love who I am.

. . . be grounded and present.

I am free to dream who I might be.

Oh my mind,
your playback
is obsolete.
No creed,
no colour,
no gender
can specify
my heartspace.
Oh my mind,
come to my
senses to
perceive
deep earth
and the
sweetness
of the
unbound
essence
of my
soul.

She wore feathers in her hair as a reminder to actively look for beauty in the lonely crowds.

Her gift was to translate what was held captive in the heart, to awaken shy strangers to self-esteem.

I have the capacity to increase my capacity.

The gift of freedom weighs
heavy on shoulders
with clipped wings.
Yet the wings of
an earth angel
regrow with every
choice that deeply
resonates with
your heart and soul.
Those wings will
grow stronger when
the inner guru
is honoured ...
and stronger still
with self respect.
An infinite soul's wings
are for soaring freely —
to the great
heights of dharma.*

* Dharma: creative destiny.

At the gate of the golden spiral the gong announces the unknown.
The cosmos bellows and groans; starlight vibrates the mind.
New waves reach the shore of your predetermined infinity,
drawing you through the mystery of pink and red creativity.
Go beyond the moon cycles that womb-man must honour,
way beyond circles that gather. Go down to the ocean,
heralded by conch, make safe passage to the island of
infinity where the new flowers of the soul bloom.

I sit on this earth humble, grateful. I listen, I bow down, I pray. I hear answers to my clarion call, I hear answers from the true guru. Ong Namo Guru Dev Namo awakens my inner teacher.

I AM
LOVE

Can you listen so very carefully that . . .

thou
lives in
the infinite

. . . you can hear the leaves of wisdom fall from trees?

Do you know your soul?
Do you ask your soul
why you are here?
Do you know you're
an earth saint?
Have you asked
your soul about the
depths of your
brilliant potential?
Have you promised
to give your soul
safe passage across
the sacred waters
of life?

You are always at the beginning of adventure, the leading edge of your being.

Sacral chakra

Second chakra, swadhisthana, pronounced 'svAA-thiSH-TAA-nuh'

Location: the area 25 mm to 50 mm below the navel

Associated body parts: sex organs, large intestine, appendix, lower vertebrae, bladder, hips

Related function: sexual, elimination, water regulation

Bija mantra, seed sound: VAM

My body holds the sacred waters — the solution for all life.
I allow these sacred waters to ebb and flow freely and be replenished.
I am here to flow with creativity.

This is the centre of your creativity, desire, emotions, sexuality and intuition. It is where you plant the seeds of creativity and learn to give and receive pleasure. This chakra stimulates the life force, other forces required for existence on the physical plane and the base of life itself. Children from the ages of 8–14 belong in this chakra. It is an age when we become established, which frees up time to explore friendships, sexuality and physical contact.

The sacral chakra is the pathway to health and youth; when it is open you will feel connected to everything. There will be a creative elegance to your accomplishments rather than a push to achieve. Insecurities around the true self — sexuality, attractiveness and feelings of inadequacy, shame and embarrassment — can be stored in the sacral chakra. Healing work in this chakra will release stagnant energy in the related areas of the body and will assist you to surrender to the creative flow of life. To create a flow of energy through this centre you can work with the breath and movement, having fun being yourself and letting go of the past. Reflect as you journal to increase awareness about where you may have judged or shamed yourself. With greater self-love you will unfurl to a greater level of self-respect, refusing to judge, blame or shame yourself, choosing instead to only encourage a sweet and natural creative self-expression to flow.

You know what is right for you and what gets your creative juices flowing. The sovereign path is to courageously follow your creative impulses for self-expression and realisation, without doubt or need for any outside approval.

What will you bloom into as the new earth is realised? What wild and precious jewel is locked within your sacral chakra? What intriguing luminosity can you bring to the surface? Through unlocking the energy in this centre, an amazing capacity for creativity and pleasure is found.

As you learn to rise from the fear-based emotions of the lower chakras and sustain your awareness through the heart, you can go even further to experience new depths of your creativity and your pleasure zones.

Swadhisthana
Sacral chakra

I pledge to honour my soul.

I will excel through any adversity.

My dharma inspires me.

My clear mind serves my pure heart.

Opportunity comes to me from all directions.

Prosperity finds me in the stream of gratitude.

One drop of the nectar of devoted love into the ocean of life is all it takes . . .

Could you, would you, will you promise to honour an infinite love affair with your soul?

I flow with creative life, I flow with divine femininity. I make marks, I draw intentions, I allow my creative impulses to flow from my singing eyes and fingers.

They will have
to readjust the
neurology of their
perception to see you.
You've really changed.
You're always in a
process of unstoppable
evolutionary change.
You are flowing
in a vibrant stream
of your evolution.

You can stop karmic wheels of repetition, cut through old cycles, dissolve negative self-talk and light up the mind with light language — positive mantras that bring a ray of infinite hope to any darkness.

I am new. I renew. I rebirth. I resurrect. My temple body is my dwelling place of sweetness where the sacred waters of creative life flow through, bringing welcomed, constant change.

Get in the flow: flowing water, flowing creativity. Answer the ringing call of divine, creative energy.

Go to the sea and play; come home to the kitchen and cook with your beloved. Enjoy yourself immensely!

Truth and beauty are invaluable; they lie within. Behold their alluring magnetism.

Let them flow unto thee; let your cup overflow.

The language of love flowed
freely from her eyes.
The language of eternity
grows from within and
unfurls unto now.
The gift of creativity cannot
be denied by those birthed
in the Age of Aquarius.
They are the water bearers
and their language
comes from the Soul.

The moment you forgive yourself and choose to be grateful for the things that grate on you — when everything changes — you become great, life feels great, you are moved towards greatness.

You are love, you are hope; you are here to birth the Age of Aquarius, the golden age, through everything you think, say and do.

Prayer of water

I go down to the water.

Down into the water.

I bow down to the water.

I pray to the sacred water.

Above and below.

I am only grateful.

Only grateful.

I am full of sweet gratitude.

I replace longing to belong with allowing my heart and soul to draw what aligns with my true self.

I let go, never pushing or grasping.

Remember: rejection is actually an experience of the universe offering you protection. Stay aligned with your heart and soul and allow the flow of the best opportunities to come to you.

Can you surrender the beginning and the end?

In tantric numerology, three is associated with the power of creativity.
Work with the power of three in every relationship. You, the other person and the energy
between you. Can you ensure this energy field is positive, compassionate, kind and creative?
And especially in a relay with Self to Self, can you create the trinity of divinity:
you, your soul and a flow of infinite divine love?

I give forth unimaginable joy. I flow with the warmth of my soul. Others seek my very good company.

I know how to listen; I know how to elevate others. My joy bubbles to the surface of my being.

Uphold your sovereignty, grace, goodness, compassion and kindness. Uphold your heart-centred dreams towards great happiness and prosperity, wealth and health.

Behold your beautiful heart and soul and never, ever turn away from your dharma. But hold on to nothing. Trust there is always abundance; let it flow, let all good things in life flow to you.

Oh, the sweetness
of the
Amrit Velā.
Oh, the sweetness
of the ambrosial
nectar.
Oh my heart flows
with creativity.
I am learning
to let go and taste
the sweetness of true
connection;
the sweet song of
life itself
flowing through
me.

Solar plexus chakra

Third chakra, manipura, pronounced 'money-poo-ruh'

Location: part of the vertebral column related to the navel region

Associated body parts: abdomen, stomach, upper intestines, liver, gall bladder, kidney, pancreas, adrenal glands, spleen, middle spine

Related function: digestion, assimilation, muscles

Bija mantra, seed sound: RAM

I am future ancient, born now. An infinite soul of love, empowered by the cosmos. Activated from the core of my true self; an invaluable, radiant, incomparable individual. I know how to serve in loving truth.

The physical centre of the third chakra is located at the navel centre, approximately 5 cm below the belly button. It is the seat of your emotions. This is the energetic centre of empowerment, self-worth, self-esteem and manifestation. In simple terms, this centre is all about self-respect.

This energy centre is the first place from which you should make decisions and take action. Sometimes you react to life, taking direction before upholding your values and responding from a place of deep self-respect.

You should move and speak from your navel point — think of it as the centre of an inner star that radiates infinite energy. Confidence is the building block and foundation of the solar plexus. This chakra contains a protective energy against any negativity that may be contained within any of the other chakras. If you do not have a strong sense of self-worth and understanding of the divinity within, the ability for self-expression will never truly manifest. Your goals may appear to have been reached, but never with a sense of fulfilment and completion if this chakra is blocked.

This energy centre relates to how you perceive yourself within society and involves ownership for the choices you make in the face of life's challenges.

Write down your very personal ambitions, listening to your gut instincts and working to honestly clear any self-concepts that are coloured by ancestry, conditioning or society.

Sight is the associated sense for the solar plexus chakra, so being clear here will bring joy to your heart. When you release all conflict in identity of self and all images of weakness, you move into an empowered state.

Always kindly evaluate yourself.

Healing the relationship you have with yourself is the foundation from which you can heal other relationships. Ensure that 100 per cent of your energy from your navel point is given to yourself first, and then you will become empowered to serve others. In your relationships be discerning and ask yourself, 'Can I be happy and free?' 'Do I feel at peace?' 'How is my heart?' 'Can I breathe happily?' 'How is my gut feeling?'

Manipura
Solar plexus chakra

Once your
solar plexus
is activated
and centred
you will burn
through all
blocks and fears
and see clearly
that you only
need to
BE you.

Could you, would you, live your dharma like your hair's on fire?

_____

_____

_____

_____

_____

_____

_____

_____

_____

_____

_____

_____

_____

_____

_____

_____

_____

_____

_____

Personal weaknesses are personal. Never put yourself down. Switch your language to positive: 'I AM . . .'

May you write your own original destiny using the language of love. You cannot be wrong; you are an eternal student of the cosmos. You get to choose your lesson plan.

Prayer of fire

May the
golden silence
that rises with
the breath of fire
bring forth
sweet wisdom.
May dancing
with the flames
of purity
burn through
all that blocks
your truth,
calm beauty and
starlit infinity.

flame

How many solar returns have you been granted? How many dances with fire and air?

Be original.

Oh my soul, I surrender my will to the long-time song of love, to the eternal dance with mystery and to the enchantment yet to be. For who am I to stand in the way of thee?

What is this precious thing that you must do? What inspired vision shows up time and time again?
What are you curiously drawn to? What longing feels so familiar and yet so new?

What awakens the soul butterflies to fly into your heart? In the quiet ambrosia hours, what loving truth is inescapable?

What nook may be found for quiet digestion?

Where may the gregarious company of this immortal coil gather?

Oh my, to sit in joy and enjoy a breath of life with good appetite.

Where do you make space to sit in candlelit candour?

How long do you make love to the evening, orchestrating time, slowing to digest?

How lovely they are: twinkling eyes, rosy cheeks fragrant lips, sweet laughter.

Note how full you can feel just to bear witness to delicate, singing fingers, spooning deliciousness.

Catch thy burning star; harness thy burning infinity into this body of divinity.

Going deeper than me, my, mine. Digging deep, surrendering, trusting . . . Thou is gold, golden, noble deep within. The ambrosial chemistry sweetens the darkness. Thine heart is gold.

When you awaken
the lioness
with the fire breath,
when you awaken
the magnificent queen
with the pure heart,
when you awaken
the deep diver
with fair spirit ...
you will discover
all treasures
beyond the beyond,
the pearl, the lotus,
the guru and infinity.
The lustrous sacredness
is always within:
go diving for pearls;
you will find them.
You are stronger,
wiser and brighter
than you think.

Once a year, when she (the sun) returns to meet your innocent heart, say yes, please, I will dance into eternity. I am radically optimistic . . .

Lift thine eyes, lift thy heart.
See clearly into a lighter fate.
Explore broad strokes;
paint only with liquid gold.
The binocular of gratitude,
the telescope of reverence,
the microscope of understanding
reveal an infinite strength within.
The golden temple shines brightly
as celestial messages ring true.
These bright visions are your dharma.
Only the noble warrior can realise
revolutionary visions of loving kindness.
Belly laugh at your fears with your north star;
good fortune forever is your good companion.

The bells are ringing. Come feast your eyes upon the sweet miracles happening now ... It is the time for courageous confidence, so ring your own bell, include yourself in celebration.

Celebrate life: light a candle, make a wish, send a prayer to your future self, send golden blessings to all.

May you be happy, may you be prosperous, may you find peace. May you honour and love your true self more and more each day.

When starlight sings
the dusty room
breathes clean.
When starlight sings
a caged soul flies
to the window
with the best view.
When starlight sings
the sound is resounding
back and forth
and now heals.
When starlight sings
the brilliance of radiance
births more love
than you know now.

Catch your burning star,
harness your burning infinity
into this body of divinity.

Heart chakra
Fourth chakra, anahata, pronounced 'un-AA-huh-THuh'
Location: heart region of the vertebrae column, centre of the chest.
Associated body parts: heart and circulatory system,
lungs, shoulders and arms, ribs/breasts, diaphragm, thymus gland.
Related function: electromagnetic-field generator, blood pressure, immunity.
Bija mantra, seed sound: YAM.
My heart is bursting with hope, courage and divine will. I embrace my
unique, rhythmic intelligence and true love for life. My heart is a wellspring
of endless joy and wisdom. My heart beats one with Mother Earth.

From the ages of 22–28 you are oriented to act from the heart space, coming to understand your life purpose and hopefully experiencing love and long-standing relationships. If you have been conditioned to judge yourself for being human or doubt your creative destiny, it may be challenging to believe in yourself. It is your birthright to be happy, living simply and learning by heart each day.

Your heart space is a very intimate and personal energetic place of refuge, connection, wisdom and individual rhythmic intelligence. As you write, imagine you are gazing into this place without limitation. Only you can see the true grace, beauty and vastness of your energetic heart and soul. This chakra is essentially the centre for the experience of purity, the joy and pleasure of true self-intimacy.

Write intimately.

Through an open heart you will understand your humanness, and from this centre you will be able to access the vision and wisdom of the upper chakras. With a heart-centred understanding of yourself you can become the muse in your life, amused by your own innocence, never ticking yourself off when you stumble or fall. When something goes wrong, you should be able to remind yourself: 'I am not wrong.'

A liberated heart is a kind and powerful tool to acknowledge necessary goodbyes for self-protection and releasing others from being bound or limited in relationship with you. Rather than be outraged by yourself or another person, the heart wisdom may offer compassion and understanding to the life journey and the myriad influences that shape each moment. Use this section of the journal to explore a deep understanding, one that may clear your own karma and use your heart energy for positive change instead of focusing on and therefore re-creating unwanted events. Using only positive nouns is very useful for opening your heart and mind to positive reconciliation and manifestation. When the lotus of the heart opens, you will access consciousness to inform you of the truth of the whole. This sweet understanding will bring respect, patience and surrender to creativity, which will lead to joy, happiness and peace.

Anahata
Heart chakra

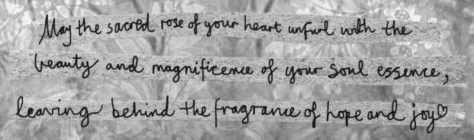

May the sacred rose of your heart unfurl with the
beauty and magnificence of your soul essence,
leaving behind the fragrance of hope and joy♡

When you invest in listening with your heart, an invaluable chain of ancient hearts opens. Can the essence of any dialogue be listening with your soul, your heart and your infinity?

'I'm not going to tell you how you should feel,' she said. With a soft smile, she then sung him a love song with her twinkling eyes and beating heart.

Can you respond to life with your creative heart? What is your response ability? Can you share the wisdom in your heart through giving forth genuine praise?

courage

hope

joy

eternal

Nourish, not punish. Breathe alive your self-belief; the deeper you breathe, the greater you will believe in your dreams, in your true spirit and in your creative potential.

love

forever

Lot

With your whole, well-nourished body keep expanding your self-belief and feel into your heart with the kind of music and songs that elevate your spirit and help to sustain your self-belief.

My heart is raj. I am unapologetic about my existence.

She swayed and danced. Refined
rawness, alive and kicking.

So very tenderly, she held the broken flowers in her warm hands. The soft fragrance of her pureness of heart bore wild and earthly stories.

the song of my heart

is so very beautiful ♡

Sing, sing, sing

I celebrate my awakened heart. ♡

Prayer of air

I call upon the sacred winds
of everlasting change,
flowing in the element of air.
Please send out this prayer
and it return to me,
over and over again . . .
so that I am awakened
in every moment
to uphold the intention
to touch the hearts
of all whom I meet;
softness of compassion,
greatness of infinity,
strength of understanding,
flexibility of patience,
humour of life,
experience of hope,
sustenance of trust,
nourishment of faith,
and always with
the language of love
from my heart.

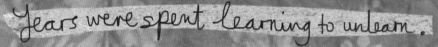

Years were spent learning to unlearn.
The heart knew all along — all tears sacred
on the tip of the artist's infinite brush.

secret
language
of the
forever
now

poetic patience

"Do kiss and tell the endless song,"
the wild, earth lovers cried. Only deeply
poetic lives satisfied the twinkling ones.

I love with the magnitude of the great cosmic beloved; within me, surrounding me, forming me. I say 'Yes!' to the divine creative energy flowing forth through me. My love is unstoppable, immeasurable.

You are supported in more ways than you can perceive.
There are said to be seven opportunities in every moment.
Just ask your heart; just ask your soul.

She didn't attempt to save time. She made sure that she spent the time in every moment doing what she'd never done before.

Throat chakra
Fifth chakra, vishuddha, pronounced 'vish-shoo-thee'
Location: throat, thyroid, trachea, neck vertebra, mouth,
oesophagus, parathyroid, hypothalamus
Associated body parts: base of the neck, throat, carotid plexus
Related function: metabolism and calcium regulation
Bija mantra, seed sound: HAM
I reach into the unknown with love. I do not stand over any other;
I listen with my heart. Before I speak I respect, connect and reflect.
I engage my rhythmic intelligence and language of my creative destiny.

The throat chakra enhances your ability to communicate, be in touch with your inner voice and be able to verbally express your deepest truth. You act from this chakra from the ages of 29–35, when you should be empowered to proclaim who you are and stand up for your true self. When you can speak kindly towards yourself and all others you are acting from the unified perspective of your heart and soul. True self-respect and awareness acknowledge the interconnectedness and value of all life on earth.

Your work here is to ensure that you are always communicating with an open heart and soul wisdom. When this chakra is open you no longer use language that separates you from receiving prosperity or that plays into victimhood. Rather than look for differences, you can acknowledge common ground because you trust in the mutuality with others. As you spiritually mature you will know that feeling superior or inferior to any other is just a trick of the ego, pulling you away from your heart.

When you connect the throat chakra to the navel point you will remain empowered and be protected and in command of the release and expression of your own energy. You will feel strong enough to make light and friendly connections without any self-compromise. Practise writing from the navel point, the physical centre of your personal power.

Using your intuition to guide you when expressing yourself, you can discern what is an authentic and self-loving tone of relay. This is useful for healthy and honest communication with others. As you write, patiently listen to your inner dialogue and allow yourself time to process what you are thinking. Self-enquire: 'Am I feeling expansive or diminished?' 'Should I pause and breathe?' These are steps that can lead to improving all of your relationships.

As you become a master of your own way of communicating you will feel the power of all words; you will feel the liberation that loving words bring — written, spoken, sung, listened to and enjoyed — without resistance. The throat chakra is the teacher and the centre where you can find healthy, authentic self-expression. When you keep listening to your inner reflections you will receive awareness of opportunities to prosper.

Vishuddha
Throat chakra

your seeds are precious, plant them

your truth
& beauty
is profound ♡

into a vibratory field of your own good intentions.

You created your future self to return to inspire you in a dream, with a beautiful truth that would only be understood when retold to a beloved. Do you remember your innocent dreams?

Prayer of ether

With my honest prayer
I reach consistently into
the unknown.
I choose to trust, believe
and hold faith.
I chant the seed sounds,
the creation sounds,
the resounding sounds of love
that can be heard deep within
the blue, blue ether.
And as these seeds
come back to me on
the sacred winds of creation,
may they fall into
the love in my heart
and grow into wisdom.
And may I share this wisdom in
the most sensitive
and compassionate ways
that lead to the joy of
a deeper, shared
understanding.

All your experiences are invaluable poetry, an aliveness that when shared, written and spoken in your own unique way becomes pages in the earth's book of everlasting love and understanding.

Soft sounds stemmed
from the golden heart
rooted in ancient soulful loving.
Whispers of innocence unbound,
forget-me-nots woven into
patterns of speech with a
longing for the language of love.

There is a truth within you, a centre point that has remained unaltered by family, education or society. Chant 'OM, OM, OM' as you dwell in your heart. Listen for your truth as it is called forth by this sound.

You can hear wishes
being fulfilled
in gentle silence,
The silence
in between
kisses.
The silence in
a loving gaze.
The silence of
sweet, soft skin.
The silence of
a loved body:
content,
calm,
rested.

The universe is a mystery, but it is not a secret.

For every question, there is an answer.

Love one another.
Bask in the light of truth
that flows through blue ether,
where all differences are
played as beautiful notes
in the same song.

Out of the blue ether,
the Atmos/Attma soul sphere,
comes the beautiful miracles
asked for from a place of love
towards love and communication
with soulful purpose.

yes please

It is through the throat chakra that you will come to true understanding. Listen to your communications and silent responses, small sounds as well as words. Connect with your 10 bodies to feel into your truth.

No
thank you!

When do you say 'Yes, please' and 'No, thank you' automatically, when perhaps the opposite or a mediated response rings true? Is there any conditioning affecting your self-expression and communication?

The enchantress offers all that she meets,

a promise of nourishment just by being in her

subtle presence; the tone of her voice, the aroma

of her body, the tranquillity of her infinite love.

Her language was universal, traversing time and space, spreading the mists of love, created by the sound current of unrelenting gratitude and praise.

In the flow of truth everything is beautifully invaluable, nothing offensive, all part of the whole.

Having the capacity to feel the totality of any given experience is often described as joy.

The truth of the universe is so immense that it is of no great benefit that you conclude anything. Conclusions lead to confusion, disillusion and being even further from the truth.

I cut through
Karmic patterns
with vibratory light
of my spoken truth.

I am grateful,
I am blessed,
I am prosperous.

Third eye chakra
Sixth chakra, ajna, pronounced 'AAg-yuh'
Location: above and between the eyebrows, medulla plexus, pineal plexus
Associated body parts: brain, nervous system, eyes,
ears, nose, pineal gland, pituitary gland
Related function: hormonal and psychological regulation
Bija mantra, seed sound: OM
I close my eyes and I see. Every moment contains seven opportunities.
I am seer, sychronised to the creative pulse, boundless and endless love,
moving through realms towards the cosmic heart. I know who I am.

This energy centre opens when you are ready to engage with your inherent wisdom. This involves a realisation of non-duality, the union of mind, body and spirit, and your connection with the universe and all that is. This centre becomes receptive when you no longer believe in the illusion of lack or victimhood and are excited to enter the deep mystery of life. The third eye is located in the middle of the forehead between the eyebrows. The 'temples' are on either side of this energy centre of intuitive power.

You are governed by the sixth chakra from the age of 36 onwards. You begin to open this energy centre whenever you feel ready to grow your awareness and see past the illusions of *maya* (material). The sixth chakra is the centre of psychic power, higher intuition, the spirit, magnetic forces and light. It is about divine thought, balanced intuition and intellect. The invisible becomes visible when you sustain awareness in this centre of higher wisdom. Spiritual fitness is improved when you keep the sixth chakra open because you are tuned in to inner guidance. When you are open to the source of all creative intelligence you allow this higher perspective to flow down through your crown chakra into your sixth chakra. As you become more practised you learn to trust the intuitive wisdom that comes through from the meditative, calm mind. In this neutral state you can allow the intellect to show you how to manifest that wisdom. We are in an age when lies and illusions are broadcast constantly. Some are so subtle that, before you are aware, they can pull your energy back down into fear-based thinking. Comparative, divisive and judgemental memes are woven through the fabric of all our communications, many creating patterns of envy and lack-based beliefs. Be watchful, know your heart and individuate. Write your insights down without the need to be right, good or better than others.

Your first tool for staying elevated is always the breath, so as you write you may like to practise breathing consciously with deep, gentle breaths; no forcing. As you become more self-aware you will witness and feel the positive power of your true self rising to overwrite past conditioning and any systems of belief that limit creative thoughts and dreams.

Ajna
Third eye chakra

there are layers beyond
layers, in layers beyond...

so just know your soul   as best as

you can 🤍

Be willing to feel the depths of

the wild journey that has no end.

let mystery

speak through the

blue, blue realm.

You didn't come into this life to 'fit in'; you came to create a new form of human expression.

NEW, NEW, NEW, NEW, NOUVEAU.

As a child you may have at times been confident, stubborn, defiant, determined, rebellious, wild and wilful as a star seed of change. See your power to effect positive change in systems that do not serve the soul of humanity and allow yourself to live by your heart and soul truth.

Engage the intelligence of your frontal lobe and heart wisdom to enter the spaces that aren't yet occupied. Imagine spaces that don't exist, as you are a pioneer of this Aquarian age.

Quieten your mind and you will see exactly where you should insert your love for all life, a celebration of diversity, respect, compassion, understanding, gratitude and universality into humanity.

vérité

truth

Why not take the best seat in the house? The third eye has the best view: 360 degrees of seer.

You are becoming a highly refined, sensory being. When you are aligned with your truth you will fly.

Many lifetimes ago she preserved the right to know her true self,

her everlasting beauty, her sweet essence, her stars and the moon in her pure, pure heart ♡

Bandages carefully unfurled, true grace radiated, so fragrant and alive.

Intuitively meet with your future self. How can you keep your wild innocence and be seer?

The opulent frequency that she mastered to uphold radiated from every cell in her being. She became magnetised for great prosperity, receiving a complex texture of opportunities, meetings, love and money better than she could imagine. With immense gratitude, she thanked the great, creative force for organising such a brilliant sequence of fortunate synchronicities on her behalf. And that was just the beginning . . .

Prayer of light

I pray to find the inner wisdom,
held safe in the ambrosia,
as the nectar releases
and the lotus rises from
strong feet at my heart.
I ground good intentions,
intertwined with true belief
in love, eternal hope and
the worth of emergent dreams.
I pray to be seer, to know how
to blaze ahead with relevant,
creative genius, co-creating
this coming golden era.
I pray to be always inspired to
work to create a bright future
as envisioned in my mind's eye.
I pray for the renaissance of
the human spirit and sweet, strong
community, alive with the delicious
rhythm of inclusive, creative life well
lived in the everlasting now.

Believe in magic? Why, my very existence is evidence of the serendipity that exists in the realms of reality.

Pinch me, hug me, laugh with me: I am a real magician. HA!

I do not know enough about anything to come to conclusions.
I resonate with the fluidity of creative love, infinitely expanding and evolving.
I write my own indigo destiny with every breath.
A fragrant rose always unfurls within the chambers of my sacred heart.

Crown chakra

Seventh chakra, sahasrara, pronounced 'suh-huss-rAA-ruh'
Location: top of the head, crown, cerebal plexus
Associated body parts: muscular system, skeletal system, skin
Related function: circadian rhythms
Bija mantra, seed sound: OM or silence.

The language of my heart is poetic and wise. Empyrean beauty animates me as I touch this earth. I exist in the infinite moment, bringing forth the light of my soul with reverence and endless gratitude. I am forever love, anew in each now. I am here now, eternal in love.

This chakra awakens when you are finally grounded and open your eyes to see that you have been led to understand life is meant for living. With maturity it is understood that living is given to you by pranic energy and there is no escaping the reality that you must live through every moment of your life regardless of how it comes to you. You are here to face the gift of life no matter what arises; this is what it means to be a noble, real and loving human.

This is a good section to practise activating your inner wisdom and then writing just as you see it, with full command of your mind: a gentle, sweet commitment to self-devotion, with the wise heart leading the way.

You become sovereign when you see the world with a sense of wonder, love and ability to sit in any discomfort — the very real nature of being imperfectly real and present while simultaneously perceiving the subtlety of the future and the forever now — as any preconceived concept of time dissolves. When this chakra is open you have no desire to escape into any fantasy. Your crown never falls off; you sit and move in a balanced way as grace personified.

You know how to have fun and belly laugh, finding humour quickly and dancing with life so that you shake and shape it, not the other way around. When you reach this ultimate, balanced state you are truly at peace with yourself and the world. You emanate love and wisdom; you are grounded and steady. Materialism and the ego (artificial intelligence) are in a paradigm you merely observe.

The keyword is 'inspiration', and this energy centre offers a higher glimpse of your role and creative destiny. It is here that you will learn to trust your inner voice, which you hear when you listen to the wisdom your future self offers. This chakra connects to an expanded, heavenly perspective where everything in this earthly reality is viewed as individuated expressions of one divine and infinite energy.

Valuing your individual, true nature is key to self-realising, as you come to be full of your soul's beautiful, vibratory truth.

Perhaps you could write in such a way that you spark the eternal love affair with your heart and soul that your humanity is for.

The lotus rises, the sacred heart rose blooms.

Sahasrara
Crown chakra

You're here in all your crowning glory! You must be in love — madly, deeply — having a wild romance self to self, as 'this is for life', you know, my dear. Promise to keep your promise?

Catch a falling star

moon woman
bright lover
its your
turn
to gently
kiss
sleeping
beauty
awake.

Humour indicates life well lived; whimsy expresses true riches; love is the invaluable currency that leads to a prosperous continuum. How are you dressing for the occasion of life?

Cosmic earthly prayer
Endless blessings,
young lovers,
moonlight drenched,
sharing,
secret nectar,
inseparable as dust,
wild lavender fields,
joyous old men,
dancing around the sun,
olive branches,
linen shirts untucked,
broad feet bare,
unstoppable women
colouring outside
of all the lines,
singing 'Hallelujah',
the yet unknown,
meeting themselves
in the ether,
falling into love,
only on earth.
Oh sweet,
lovely everything,
blessings for you,
tasting the fullest life
as you sip sweet *prana*
with no resistance at all.
Thank you for wisely
bringing heaven to earth.
Endless blessings to you
and you and YOU!

The wise let go of all
cultural divides,
seeing the magic
in the diverse
and imaginative
verses yet to be
told in the stories
that create this
universe and,
indeed, the
megaverse.

Witness others, see them, propel them into their creative destiny with your belief ~ You could decide to become the miracle bringer - it's possible!

Life has a flow when dreams are held tenderly, when there is space for potential, never the attitude of limitation. To limit spirit is impossible, to limit love creates distance from ease, dis-ease. Let love live through you.

Your human sovereignty
is universally coveted,
an auspicious embodiment
of true, free spirit with
infinite possibilities; dream
weaver, future bringer,
imagination igniter,
visionary of joy,
poet of enchantment,
solution presenter.
Never say never.

infinite

Possibilities

What flows from my mind grows into my life. I meditate to command my mind to be steady and strong, aligned with my heart and open to the wisdom of the universal mind.

Command your mind to stretch, to go beyond the old matter of fact into the realms of sacred dream time and imagining the new — to the highest spheres of heaven to make love real.

There are landscapes you've yet to explore . . . See them, envision them in the dream state with the meditative mind and the buoyant heart.

That loving feeling disappears when you move away from a heart-mind connection and your thought processes go to the back of the mind: the old cupboard filled with 'bored' games, with boring rules.

There is a golden spiral of creativity
that propels the universe to grow,
so while you are bound to honour
the earth's natural cycles
you are also encouraged to stretch out
and create anew.
The ritual of consistently and continuously
honouring cycles creates a container
for the fragrance
of your soulful visions to alchemise.
The transits of planets beckon you to release
your potent dreams for realisation.
Working with natural law, you
can vibrate the cosmos.
From the altitude of gratitude
and invincibility,
everything you need for your
creativity to bloom will come to you.

Aura
Eighth chakra, pronounced 'OR-rah'
Location: lies within your physical body then
extends out from your body in an egg shape.
A healthy aura extends up to 2.7 metres.
Related function: projection, protection.
I project luminous radiance and creative thoughts.
I am the light of my soul, respectfully contained.
I am protected by my own positive energy field.
I am blessed and supported in all four directions, above and below.

From the state of a strong, calm mind you may become more interested in inner harmony, understanding more clearly how inner peace can create profound healing in every direction. In the neutral mind you may observe there is really no right or wrong, just different perspectives and experiences thereof. A clear intention to self-protect leads to a certain detachment from the world's drama.

Every individual living in self-respecting harmony, gently grounded, projecting calm presence in the here and now, is contributing to collective harmony and peace on earth.

Your eighth chakra is a living entity, the fingerprint of your soul, the light of your truth and a measurable field of electromagnetic energy that surrounds your body. Everything in existence, even atoms, creates an encircling energetic field. You have the ability to strengthen and fine tune your own magnetic field by continuously attuning to your natural rhythmic intelligence, and therefore uniting the male and female energies within.

Once you begin to integrate your totality and keep your chakras clear, the aura may radiate your unique personal frequency. When the aura is clear of subconscious garbage your ability to perceive and receive all energy is more refined. A healthy aura requires knowing yourself with an ability to discern and clearly respect personal boundaries. A powerful eighth chakra is as noble as gold, automatically deflecting and filtering negative influences and radiating your magnetic vibrancy. If you behave in a diminished way your aura will be weakened and you will become more vulnerable to viruses and the negative and aggressive attitudes of others.

Here is a mantra for the aura: 'I am contained, committed and continuously self-renewing within a clear, personal field of creativity, compassion and calm.'

This section of the journal is an opportunity to reflect on where you may set intentions to have healthy boundaries.

You are a wonderful, living solution, naturally imaginative and original, so allow yourself to daydream on a regular basis: to imagine your life unfurling with fragrance, harmony and rhythmic intelligence. Where may you dare to individuate with whimsy creativity?

What you offer in love will return with love.

Aura
Eighth chakra

Believe in your dreams with all your love and blessings, and tend to them in your magnetic fields (the heart and aura). Grow your dreams as real, letting magnetic magic attract the opportunities to realise them.

Astral prayer

I pray to love and
understand my
physical body so
that I am always
well nourished.
Knowing that from
this place of deep
nourishment, I am open
to infinite possibilities.
I pray that I can
release all negativity
out of my aura so that
I can clearly project
my heart dreams with a
clarion call.
I pray that I am
listening when the
answers return.
I pray that I continue to
believe and rely upon
miracles.
As I attune the
instrument of my
body to refined
expression, I trust
that the sweet music
of my life on earth will
bring forth great astral
wisdom and beauty for
me to realise here
and now.

What is wanting you to discover it?

You've never been right here before, ever! This is a brand new moment, a golden opportunity and far greater than the old world can comprehend. Old perceptions only see old movies.

love is the golden rule

Sometimes you just need some quiet time, some solitude, to be centred and still, to strengthen and clear your auric field.

Go and sit under a tree and download some wisdom that comes from the heart of the earth.

Let the thinking mind turn off for just awhile.

You are so beautiful to me, so very, very beautiful, I imagine you as I write. I see you, this is for you.

Harmony, peace, forgiveness, understanding, sharing, compassion, creativity, love.

Grace, radiance, nobility, kindness, sovereignty, strength; imaginative, wild love.

In stillness, I serve.
In silence, I listen.

Can you be such a diplomat that you only project the blessings you want to return to you?

Your projection should be your protection. Refine, refine, refine.

I am hyper-synchronised with the dimensions where magic is real. I am always in the right place at the right time.

I am stronger than I think. The ability to make real progress is only hindered by the mind. I alchemise karma into dharma. I am seer of my destiny; I know where the fun is to be had. I am an unstoppable soul of love.

Love is space, the space to change. Change is stability and stability is change.
Everlasting love changes everything.

Write yourself a love letter. Make it really mean something from your heart to your soul.
Make a promise, make a wish. Your dharma is a promise to fulfil.